EVERYDAY AI

INTERACTING WITH ARTIFICIAL INTELLIGENCE

by Tammy Enz

CAPSTONE PRESS
a capstone imprint

Published by Capstone Press, an imprint of Capstone
1710 Roe Crest Drive, North Mankato, Minnesota 56003
capstonepub.com

Library of Congress Cataloging-in-Publication Data is available on the Library of Congress website.

ISBN: 9798875254000 (hardcover)
ISBN: 9798875253959 (paperback)
ISBN: 9798875253966 (ebook PDF)

Summary: Voice assistants. Smart boards. Video game opponents that seem to learn your moves. Artificial intelligence is everywhere . . . even in places you might not expect! Explore how AI is shaping everyday life—from classrooms and hospitals to entertainment and transportation.

Editorial Credits:
Editor: Donald Lemke; Designer: Bobbie Nuytten; Media Researcher: Svetlana Zhurkin; Production Specialist: Whitney Schaefer

Image Credits:
Getty Images: Francesco Carta fotografo, 22, Hispanolistic, 11, Hulton Archive/Central Press/Jimmy Sime, 8, LumiNola, 14, mikimad, 15, Oscar Wong, 10, Pollyana Ventura, 4, portishead1, 5, Tara Moore, 26, vorDa, 24; Shutterstock: aleks333, 16, Ann in the uk, 27, Best-Backgrounds (computer code), cover and throughout, Deemerwha studio, 29, DenPhotos, 9, Dusan Petkovic, 13, Gorodenkoff, 7, 18, Ground Picture, 17, Krakenimages, cover (middle), Master Video, 19, metamorworks, 21, 23, Nan_Got, 20, otsphoto, 25, Roman Samborskyi, 6, SkillUp, cover (top) and throughout, Tint Media, 28, Wassenbergh, 12

Printed and bound in China. PO 6459

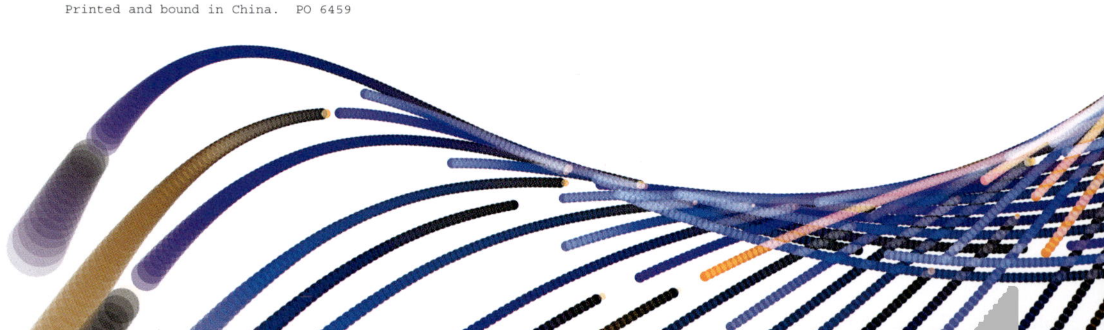

Table of Contents

CHAPTER 1

What Is AI?

Tommy was having trouble with his math homework. He didn't understand how to solve one of the problems. His mom showed him a new app she had downloaded onto her phone. It was powered by AI, or artificial intelligence.

Tommy typed in the problem. The AI program gave him a hint and then demonstrated how to solve the problem, step-by-step. The app even checked his answer! Tommy finished his homework quickly and felt proud of what he'd learned.

AI tools like this help kids every day. They can check spelling, explain tricky math problems, and suggest ideas for science projects. AI-powered programs learn from experience—just like people do. The more they're used, the better they get.

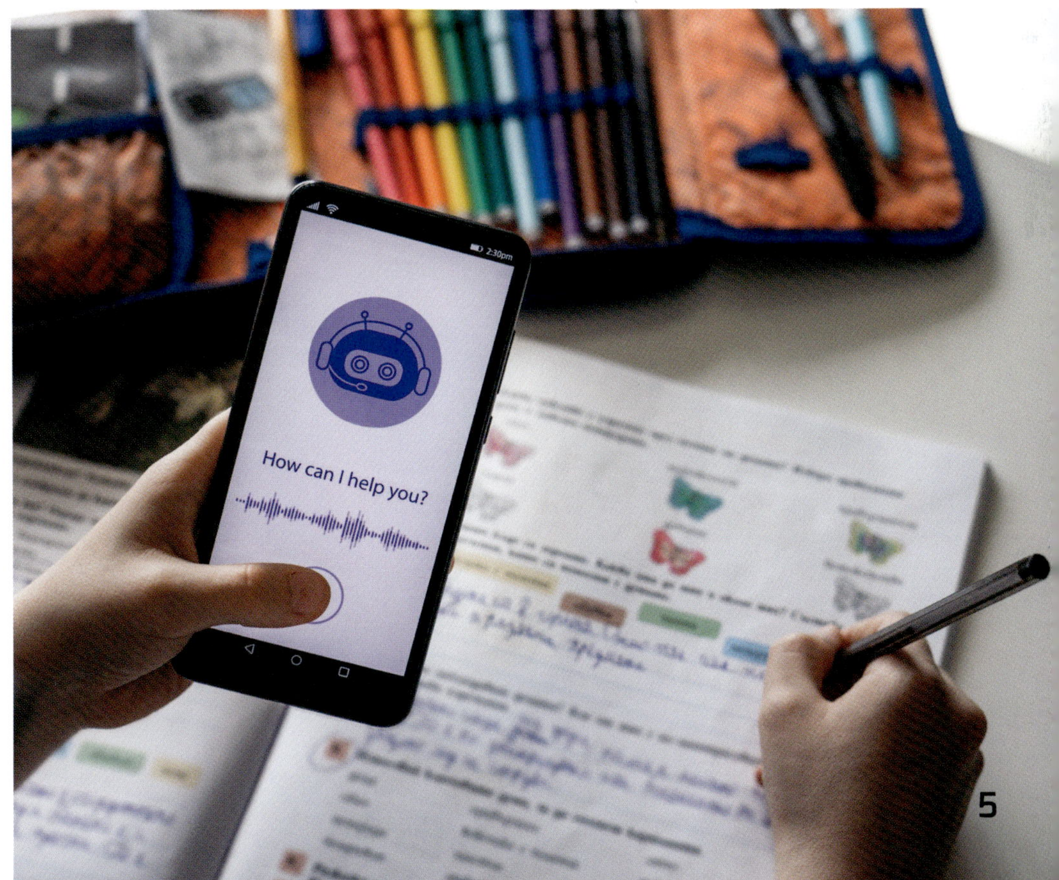

AI stands for artificial intelligence. This phrase means machines like computers or robots can do things that usually require human thinking. They learn, solve problems, and make decisions.

You've probably already used AI. Smart assistants, like Siri or Alexa, use AI to answer questions or set timers. Games and apps use AI to recommend TV shows, suggest moves, or respond to your actions.

How does AI work? This technology uses something called data. That's information—like pictures, numbers, or words. The more data AI receives, the better it gets at figuring things out. It continually learns from new data, just like you learn from new experiences.

AI has been around for a long time. In fact, scientists started exploring AI back in the 1950s! They wanted to build machines that could think, solve problems, and even play games like chess.

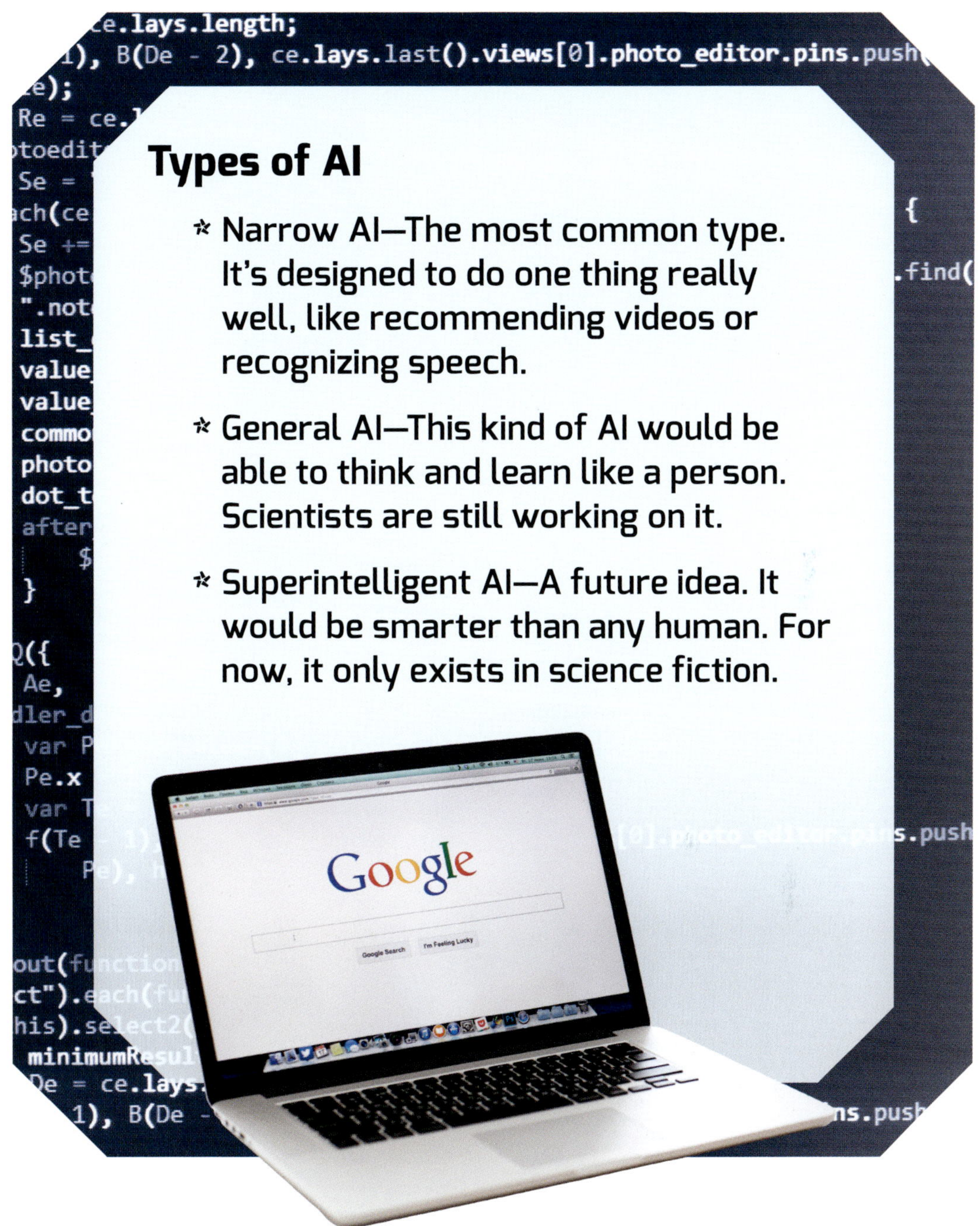

Types of AI

- Narrow AI—The most common type. It's designed to do one thing really well, like recommending videos or recognizing speech.
- General AI—This kind of AI would be able to think and learn like a person. Scientists are still working on it.
- Superintelligent AI—A future idea. It would be smarter than any human. For now, it only exists in science fiction.

AI is already part of everyday life. From smartphones to cars to schoolwork apps, AI helps us learn, play, and stay organized.

CHAPTER 2

AI at Home

At home, AI is everywhere! Smart speakers, like Alexa or Google Assistant, can tell you the weather, play music, or answer your questions.

Many homes have smart lights that turn on automatically or thermostats that adjust the temperature. AI even helps keep homes safe. Smart security systems use AI-powered cameras and motion sensors to detect unusual activity and send alerts.

Even your fridge might use AI to remind your family when you're low on milk!

AI makes everyday life easier—and more fun! Do you like watching movies? Streaming apps, like Netflix, use AI to suggest shows you might like based on what you've already watched.

AI helps with chores too. Robot vacuums, like Roomba, use AI to clean your home. They move around furniture and learn the best path through each room.

Some smartwatches use AI to track your steps, monitor sleep, and remind you to move or drink water. AI helps you stay healthy even while you sleep!

CHAPTER 3

AI at School

AI is changing how we learn. Some classrooms use AI tutors that help with math, reading, or science. These tools explain things in different ways so students can understand.

AI also helps teachers. Some AI programs track student progress and highlight those who need extra help. That way, teachers can adjust lessons to support each of their students.

AI tools can also improve your writing. They help spot spelling or grammar mistakes and suggest clearer sentences.

Did You Know?

Speech-to-text programs turn spoken words into writing. They're great for students who have trouble typing!

AI helps with reading as well. Some AI-powered apps listen to students read and help them sound out hard words. These apps change the level of difficulty to match a student's ability. If a student has trouble with a word, the program gives them more practice. If a student does well, the program gives them harder words to try.

In some classrooms, AI tracks how students are doing with assignments. The technology gives quick feedback so students know if they made a mistake and can fix it right away. This helps students learn from their mistakes and get better.

Did You Know?

Apps like Duolingo and Babbel use AI to teach new languages. They even use chatbots to help you practice conversations!

CHAPTER 4
AI for Health

AI is also helping doctors take better care of patients. One way is by looking at medical images, like X-rays. Doctors sometimes miss small changes in these high-tech pictures, but AI can spot these changes quickly and accurately. This helps doctors make better choices about how to take care of you.

AI is also used in hospitals to watch over patients. Some AI systems track heart rate, breathing, and body temperature. If something seems wrong, AI programs can let doctors and nurses know right away.

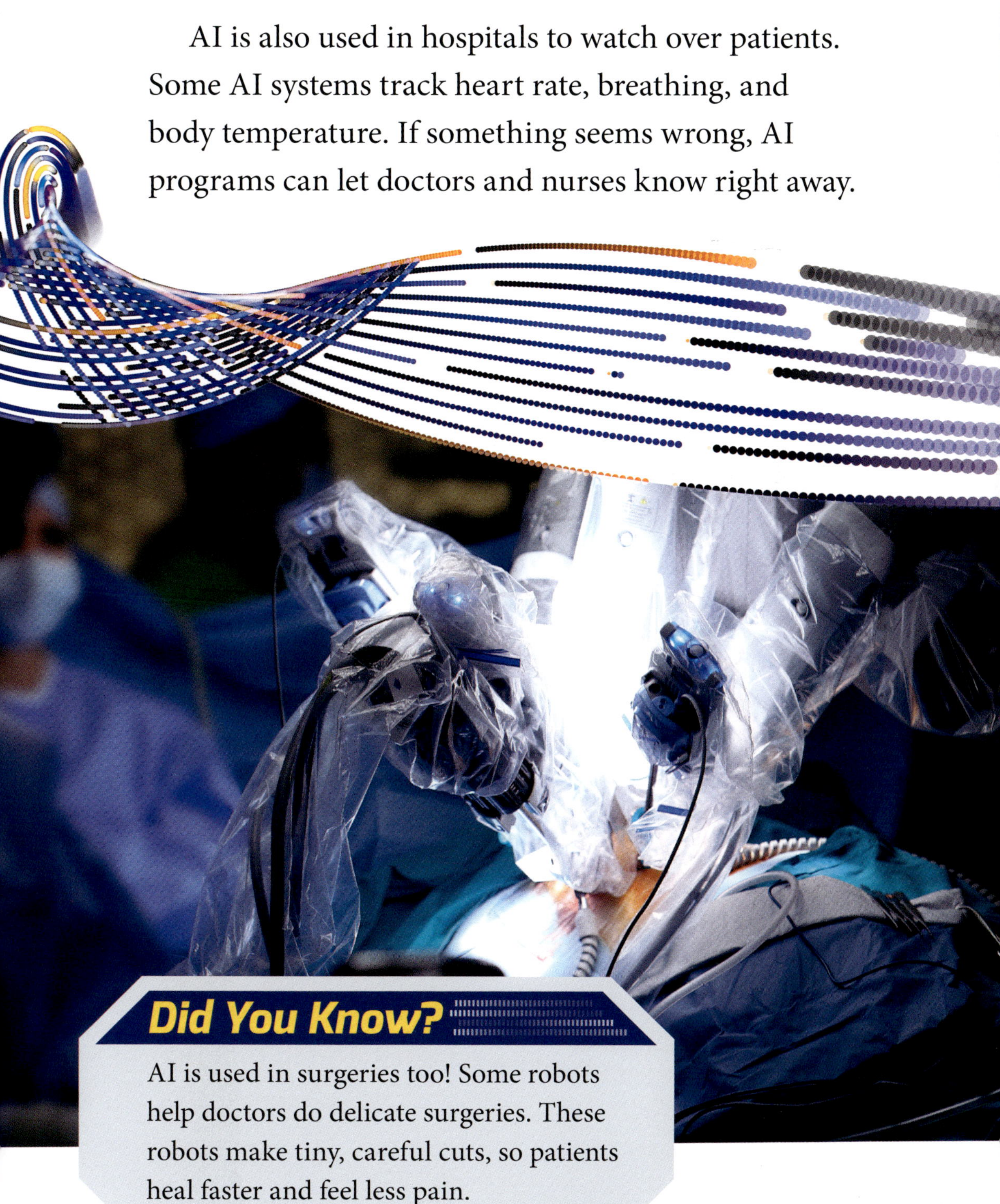

Did You Know?

AI is used in surgeries too! Some robots help doctors do delicate surgeries. These robots make tiny, careful cuts, so patients heal faster and feel less pain.

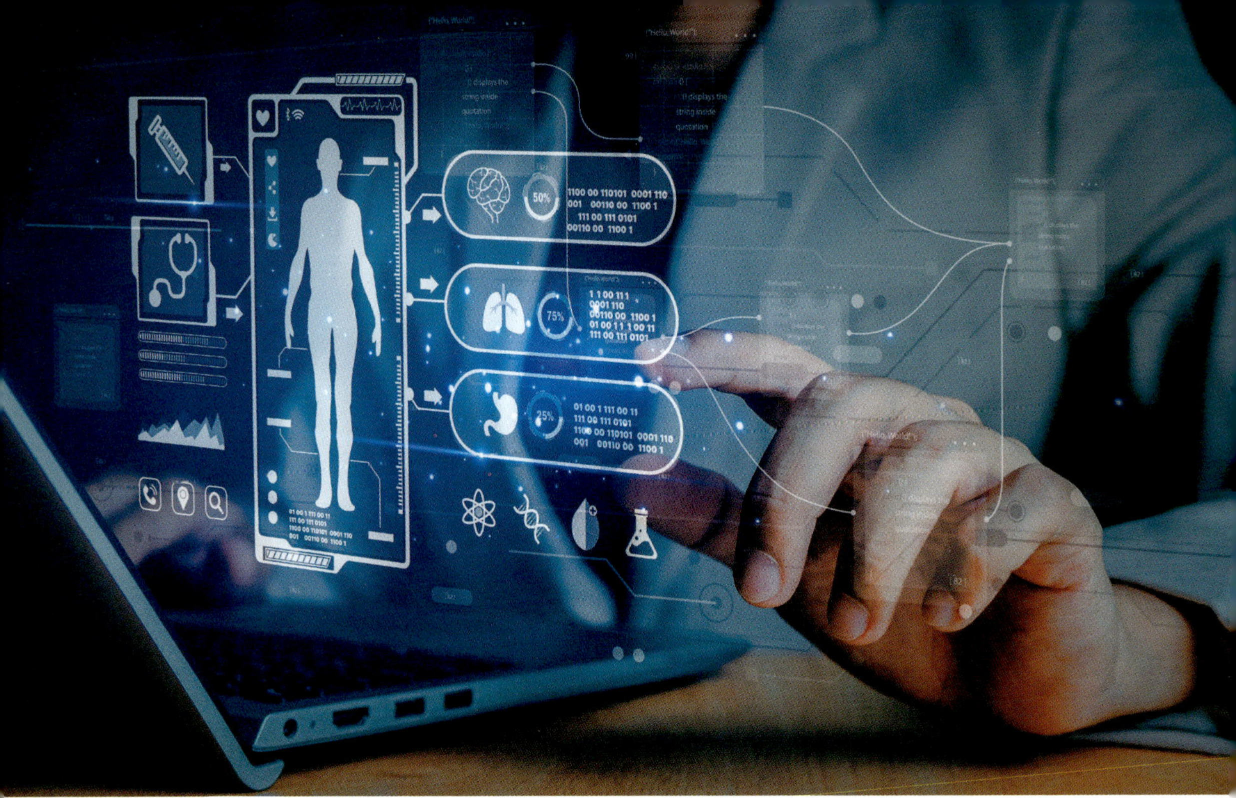

Besides helping doctors, AI is making healthcare better in other ways. For example, some hospitals are using AI to predict which patients might get sick in the future. By looking at health data, AI can spot patterns and warn doctors before symptoms show up. This early warning allows doctors to treat patients faster, which can save lives.

AI is also being used to help with drug discovery. It can look through huge amounts of data to find the best treatments for diseases. This helps scientists find cures faster and more accurately. In some cases, AI has even helped discover new medicines.

As AI becomes more advanced, it will play a bigger role in healthcare, helping doctors, nurses, and patients. It can make medical treatments safer, faster, and more personal, which is good news for everyone!

Did You Know?

Scientists at Stanford University developed Evo 2. This AI program analyzes DNA samples. DNA makes the building blocks inside the cells of all living things. AI's analysis can predict when diseases like cancer might happen.

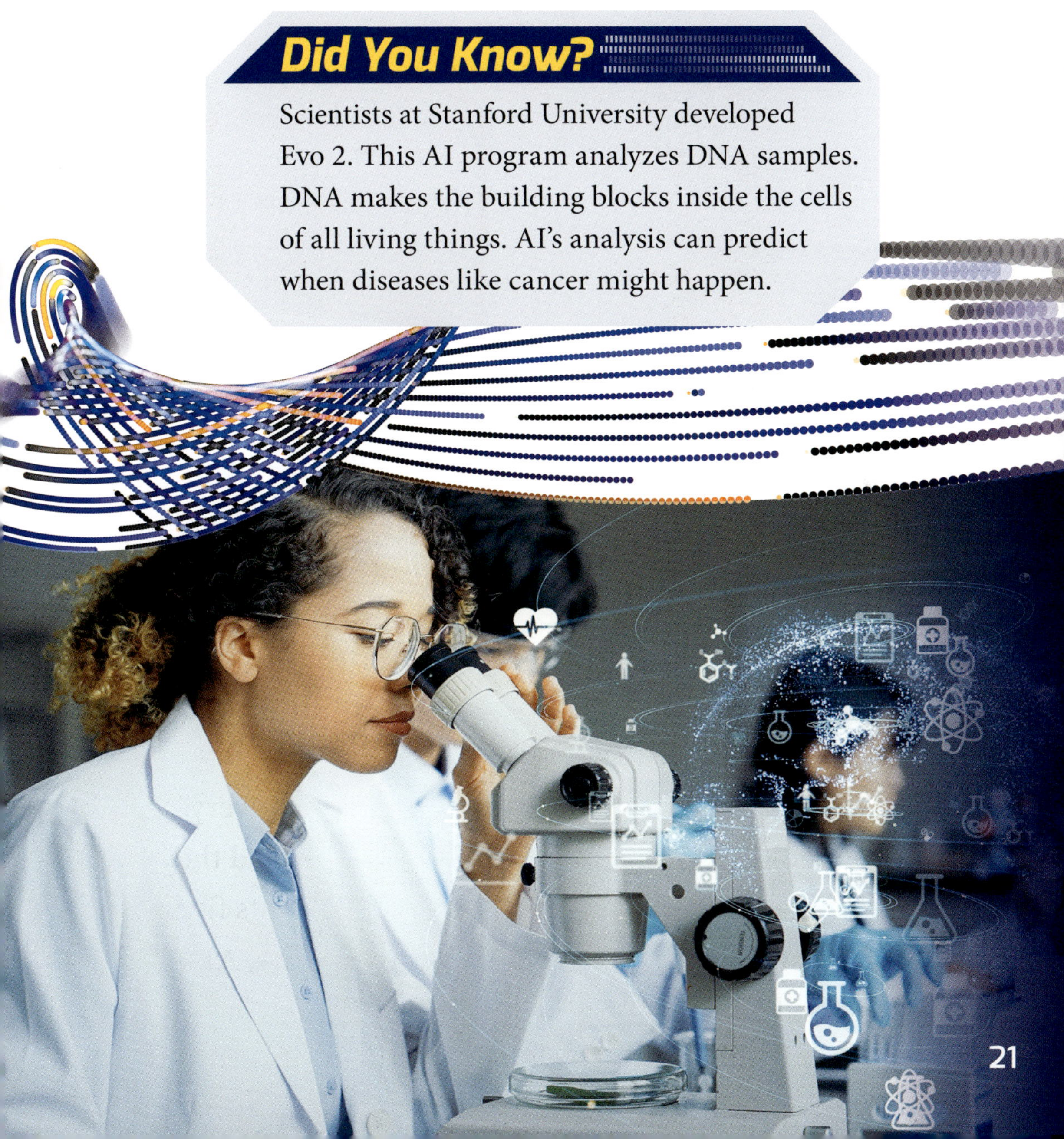

CHAPTER 5

AI and You

AI helps with everyday tasks. It can answer questions, organize your schedule, and help with schoolwork—all in seconds.

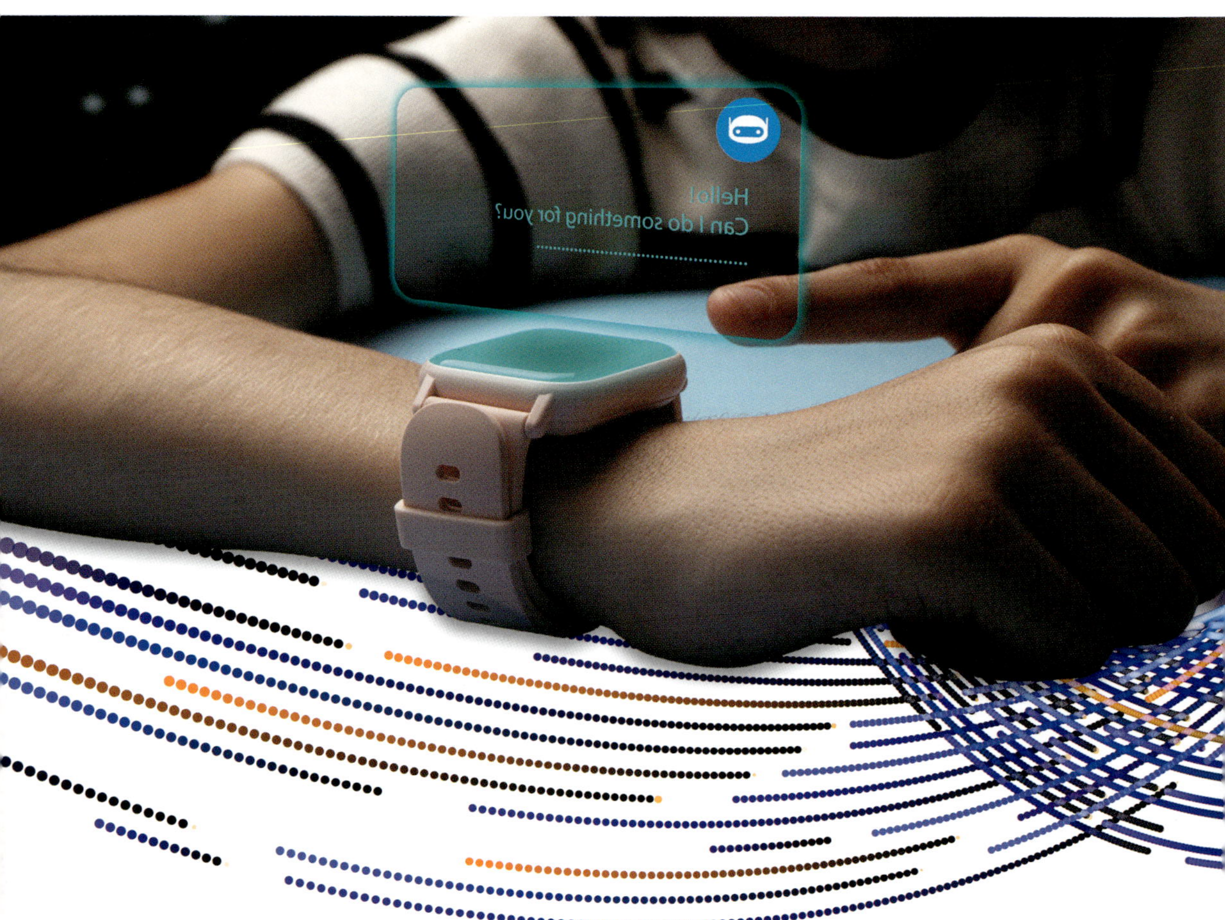

AI might even help you plan your week! Some assistants can suggest meals or help you stay healthy by picking recipes with your favorite foods.

AI is also part of transportation. Self-driving cars use AI to follow the road, obey traffic signals, and avoid accidents. In the future, more of these cars may be on the roads, making travel safer.

Did You Know?

The first self-driving car was invented in 1925! It could start its engine, shift gears, and use the horn—all by radio control. But unlike AI cars, it didn't make driving decisions on its own.

AI can also help you make new friends. That's right! Some apps use AI to help find other kids who like the same things you do, like playing sports, games, or even listening to music. The LEGO Play app allows LEGO fans to find friends and play games. Another app called Snap Map uses AI to help kids find their friends anywhere on the planet.

AI can also help you find lost pets. If your pet goes missing, some smart collars can help you track where they are. Whistle Go and PawTrack are collars that use AI to find lost pets. They also track your pet's health. They use AI to alert you to problems. They can even help find vet care for cats and dogs.

With AI, you can find new friends and make sure your pets are safe!

AI is a helpful tool, but it's important to use it safely. Before using AI apps or devices, always ask a caretaker or teacher. There are many cool AI tools that can help you with schoolwork, projects, and games. You can use AI to research topics for school. You can use it to practice a new language or improve your drawing skills.

But, just like any tool, it's important to be careful when using AI. Be sure to use it for good things and avoid sharing personal information online.

Did You Know?

AI can also help you get creative. There are apps that use AI to turn your drawings into cartoons. Other AI apps help you create new music or stories.

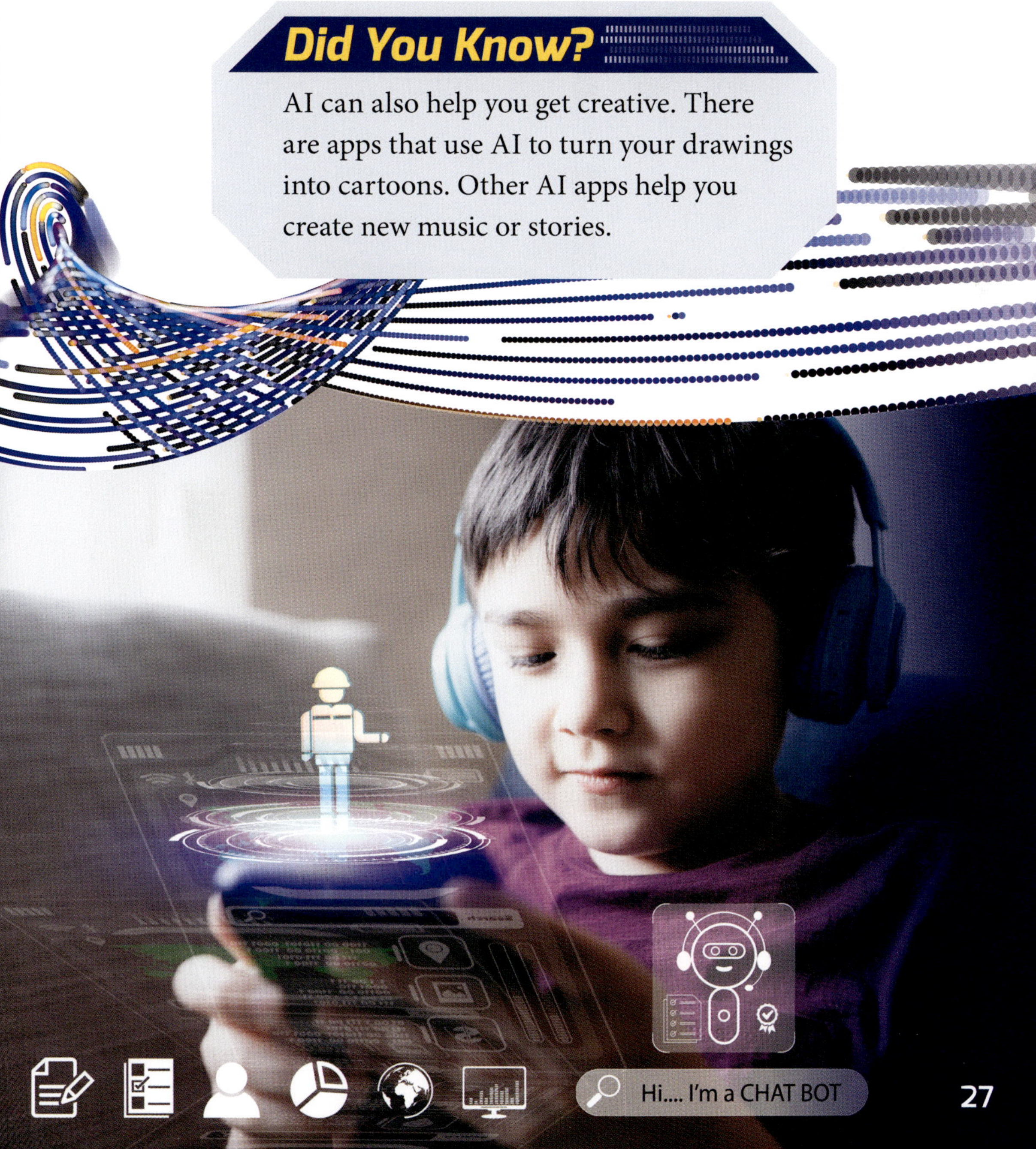

The world of AI is growing, and the future is full of exciting possibilities. What might AI be able to do in the future? Maybe it will help astronauts explore space or help people create amazing art. It could even help us solve some of the world's biggest problems, like climate change or poverty.

AI will keep changing and getting better. As you learn more about it, you might find new ways to use AI to make the world a better place. So, keep learning, stay curious, and always think about how you can use technology to make the world better.

Key AI Search Terms

1. AI for Kids
2. Artificial Intelligence Education
3. AI Learning Tools
4. AI in School
5. AI for Social Media Safety
6. AI and Privacy for Children
7. AI and Online Safety

Internet Sites

Britannica Kids: Artificial Intelligence
kids.britannica.com/kids/article/artificial-intelligence/390648

Code.org: Explore Learning for Ages 5 to 11
Code.org

ISTE: Artificial Intelligence in Education
iste.org/ai

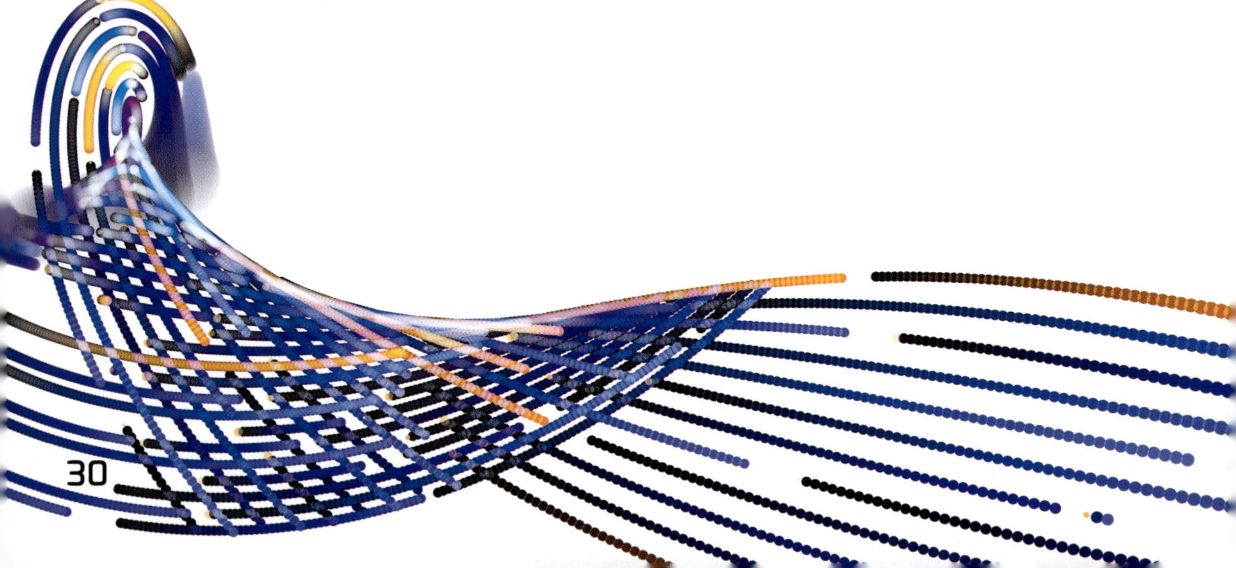

Glossary

app (AP)—a program or tool on a phone, tablet, or computer that helps you do something, like play games or learn new things

artificial intelligence (ahr-tuh-FISH-uhl in-TEHL-uh-juhns)—computers or robots that can think, learn, and solve problems like people

assistant (uh-SIH-stuhnt)—a helper that can do tasks or answer questions, like Siri or Alexa

data (DA-tuh)—information, like pictures or numbers, that computers use to make decisions or learn

feedback (FEED-bak)—information or advice about how well something is done, so you can improve

program (PROH-gram)—a set of instructions that tells a computer what to do

robot (ROH-bot)—a machine that can do tasks or work by itself, sometimes with help from AI

sensor (SEN-sohr)—a device that can see, hear, or feel things, like a camera or microphone

technology (tek-NAH-luh-jee)—tools or machines made to solve problems or make life easier, like computers or robots

virtual (VUR-chuh-wuhl)—something that seems real but is actually done or seen through a computer or phone screen

Index

About the Author

Tammy Enz holds a bachelor's degree in civil engineering and a master's degree in journalism and mass communications. She works as a structural engineer and teaches at the University of Wisconsin-Platteville. She has written dozens of books on science and engineering topics for young people.